HEADSTRONG GIRL

WRITER CHAPS – SEASON ONE

SHORT BOOKS FULL OF OUTSTANDING ADVICE FROM AUSTRALIA'S TOP SPECULATIVE FICTION WRITERS

You Are Not Your Writing and Other Sage Advice, Angela Slatter

From Baby Brain To Writer Brain: Writing Through A World of Parenting Distractions, Tansy Rayner Roberts

Eyes on the Stars: Writing Science Fiction & Fantasy, Sean Williams

The Martial Art of Writing and Other Essays, Alan Baxter

Capturing Ghosts on the Page, Kaaron Warren

Headstrong Girl: How To Live A Writer's Life, Kim Wilkins

HEADSTRONG GIRL

How To Live A Writer's Life

KIM WILKINS

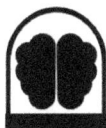

Brain Jar Press
PO Box 6687
Upper Mt Gravatt, QLD, 4122
Australia
www.BrainJarPress.com

Cover design by Peter Ball
Cover Images: angry woman grinding teeth with speech bubble, durantelallera/Shutterstock

ISBN: 978-1-922479-16-7 (Print); 978-1-922479-17-4 (Ebook)

Contents

Introduction   vii

The Writing Life   1

The Romance Of Work   3
Eight Years Old Again   5
Other People   7
Don't Get Up   9
The Joys Of Being A Plotter   11
Your Writing Fitness   14
Multi-millionaire   16

The Craft Of Writing   19

Plot Versus Character   21
Building Blocks   23
Narrative Structure   25
Managing Scope   27
Four Ways To Get To Know Your Characters   29
Your Supporting Cast   31
World Building   33
Orient And Anchor   35
What To Do About Clichés   37
Calendar Of Events   39
Precision Editing   41
Keep Going   43

About the Author   45

Introduction

This little book contains what I'd let someone else call 'all my writing wisdom'. I have called it *Headstrong Girl* because, as a child, that was my favourite kind of character. Headstrong girls always knew which direction to go, they had strong moral compasses, and sure people thought they were bossy but more often than not they were right.

When it comes to writing, more often than not, I am right.

But I would say that... I'm quite headstrong.

The first part of the book is a collection of short pieces on the writing life. They are not particularly recently written, because they are drawn from my social media and I gave up on social media a few years back: because I am headstrong and I think social media is the biggest fucking waste of anybody's time and mental energy, and especially for a writer. I have chosen pieces that I still stand by, and refreshed them if they seemed dated.

The second part of the book is a collection of columns on the craft of writing. These are all aspects of craft I still teach, when I teach (which is not as often as it used to be). They are intended to be useful little tips and tricks that will improve your writing *right this instant*.

I would say that my 'writing wisdom' may very well have developed since some of these short pieces and columns were written. If anybody asked me for my best writing advice now, I would probably say something like: Don't mythologise your writing; have a much more workmanlike and practical relationship with it. Have a writing buddy who is working at approximately the same level as you who'll give you honest feedback. Read a lot more; some writers think if they see a lot of Marvel movies they can write a good book and that's probably not true (those things aren't mutually exclusive: I love Marvel movies and I like to think I write good books, but I don't learn a lot about writing craft from Marvel movies). Most of all, for God's sake, don't use the hashtag #amwriting. If you are using the hashtag #amwriting you're fucking lying. You're on Instagram. I can see it.

The path to happiness in writing is always in the *process*: the imagining and the writing. And maybe your writing doesn't even matter as much as you think it does. There are so many ways to use your imagination and be happy. Daydreaming. Playing games. Talking shit with friends.

For what it is worth, though, what follows is a headstrong girl's take on the writer's life, should you wish to take that path. Godspeed!

The Writing Life

The Romance Of Work

When I was a little girl, I read a book that would affect me profoundly. It was Gladys Malvern's *The Dancing Star*, first published in 1942, an account of the life of Anna Pavlova, written for children. Like many little girls, I dreamed of being a ballet dancer but unfortunately I was very, very bad at dancing and didn't progress beyond the one disastrous Christmas concert (let me just say: if you're a blue fairy and you're with the pink fairies when you're not supposed to be, you stand out). But it wasn't the stuff about ballet that affected me so deeply, it was the stuff about work.

According to the book, Anna Pavlova was obsessed with dancing. She practised all the time. She did it until her toes bled and she just... kept... going. This notion, that one could work so hard and push through barriers of extreme discomfort, really took hold of my imagination. From that moment on, I understood the incredible romance of work: diligent hours spent on something that mattered to make an outcome appear in the world.

This is why I don't hold much with the myth of inspiration: the idea that somehow you must have about yourself the perfect set of preconditions for creativity to be bestowed upon you by a muse. Coleridge stopped writing 'Kubla Khan' when a 'gentleman from Porlock' stopped by on some business or another, and interrupted his flow of inspiration (Coleridge clearly never had responsibility for small children, who are magnificent porlockers). The myth of inspiration is pleasantly mystical, I suppose, but it isn't nearly so effective as work.

So work in the early morning hours when the family is asleep. Work until late when the words are flowing. Work on a freshly printed manuscript with a brand new pen while it rains outside. Work when it all seems too hard and your metaphorical toes are bleeding and you have to push through the pain. Work on something you care about so passionately that, like a new lover, you can't leave it alone. Art, when viewed in this light, is not a divine bolt from above, but the sweet, constant labour of real human beings manifesting things with their feet in the soil. And there is no idea about art more pleasing to me than that.

Eight Years Old Again

About a year ago, I dreamt that I found an old notebook with outlines and ideas for a story I was writing when I was eight. On the cover was a yellow-and-gold-toned photograph of the sea at sunset, and inside was lots of my loopy, girlish writing. Finding this notebook filled me with impossible bliss. I'd found it! That thing that made me happier beyond all other happinesses! When I woke in the grey dawn, I almost wept. That pleasure of putting stories together as a child was what had driven me to write for most of my life. But becoming a published author (or, in my case, two published authors) and having deadlines to manage, not to mention a job to hold down and children to raise, had recently made writing a task to be scheduled into a busy life. Often, I would sit down feeling distracted and despondent, and take a good half hour to get any momentum. I was still writing, still enjoying my stories, but it wasn't like in the dream, where it was the most perfect joy of them all.

That dream made me revisit my priorities. It's taken some time and some tough calls, but right now I am writing the sequel to *Daughters of the Storm* (tentatively called "A Sea of Wings" and yes, it is mostly set by the seaside, just like the photograph on the cover of my dream-notebook), and the feeling is back! I wake up itching to write. The story is playing in my head like a movie the whole time. The solution all along was to make time and space in my mind all throughout the day, rather than forcing myself only to think about the story in the small windows of time I had to write. I'm writing reams and reams and it's massaging my soul; I'm so happy. I'm even getting great ideas for the next book, so I'm hoping to continue riding this wave for a long time to come.

Remember, kids: know the difference between what is urgent and what is important. Writing is the most important thing that I do. Everything else can wait a little while.

Other People

When I worked on a monthly writing advice column, I asked some friends to suggest topics, and was very interested to see a set of questions crop up about how to manage interactions with others while working on your writing. The stereotypical image of a writer is somebody who works alone for long uninterrupted stretches of time, who then emerges with a complete manuscript independently. The truth is, writers have to rely on others for help and support—family, friends, professional contacts—and managing those relationships will make your writing career run much more smoothly.

HOW DO YOU TELL YOUR FRIENDS AND FAMILY YOU ARE WRITING A BOOK?

You must be prepared to specify what you see as their role in your writing life. Your mother may want to read what you've written thus far with a critical eye. Your ungrateful teenage children may prefer you spend your writing time driving them to parties. Your best friend may ring you daily to ask how much you've written to 'put some pressure' on you. So you should say up front, 'I am writing a book, and what I need from you is...'. Try not to demand too much. Remember what Stephen King says in *On Writing*: 'life is not a support system for art; it's the other way around.'

HOW DO YOU KNOW IF SOMEBODY IS GIVING YOU GOOD CRITICISM?

This is tricky, because nobody likes to be criticised, so our default setting is to want to reject criticism when it comes along. But there are some things you can look out for. Does this person read in the genre? If not, their criticism is of limited use. Do you get a sense of the person enjoying their power over you too much? If so, their criticism may be harsher than necessary. The best criticism will usually resonate with you the strongest. It will articulate that weakness you thought you'd managed to hide or gloss over. It will make you uncomfortable rather than wounding you mortally.

HOW DO YOU SURVIVE WRITER ENVY?

If somebody else you know is a very good writer, that doesn't mean they could write your story better than you. Nobody is more qualified to write your story than you, because it came out of your head. If your envy is attached to a writer's public or financial success, remember Anne Lamott's fabulous advice in *Bird by Bird*: never compare how you feel on the inside, to the way somebody else looks from the outside. I know plenty of miserable rich and successful people. You'd be better off adopting a dog if happiness is your goal.

HOW CAN YOU ASK PEOPLE TO HELP WITHOUT BEING PUSHY?

By being frank. You tell them that you are uncomfortable about asking, and you tell them you will understand if they say no. You honour their time, and you promise to pay it forward. And one day, when you are a bigshot writer, somebody will ask you for help. So keep your promise.

Don't Get Up

Shit just got real around here, with me needing to start a new Kimberley Freeman, finish my novella collection, and write an academic paper. It's a big scary bottleneck of WRITE SOMETHING, BITCH so I've had to have a long hard look at my writing habits, which have been a bit slippery of late.

We all understand that to write we have to sit at our keyboards (for example, I'm sitting at mine right now, in bed with the electric blanket on … this is my favourite way to work). But I don't think sitting at the keyboard is specific enough advice anymore. Do you know why? Because of the siren call of the FUCKING internet, which clearly doesn't want me to get my work done.

Because in every writing project — creative or otherwise — there comes a moment where you hit a slow spot and you're not quite sure what to write next. Now at this stage, many of us will pop open an internet browser. Guess what, you just walked away from the work. You just got up and walked away. Worse: you just put your writing out of your head too. At least if you take a little walk around your garden, you can still be mulling it over. Let me make this really clear to you:

- When you Google a bit of research, you have walked away from your work and are now in a library. That's kind of okay, but it's a library where there are a lot of celebrity gossip mags lying around that have enticing headlines.

- When you open Facebook, you have walked away from your work and are now in a room full of your friends and they are all bored and talking derp and exchanging hilarious animal pictures.
- When you start instant messaging, you have walked away from your work to chat with a friend.
- When you slide over to your favourite blogs, you have walked away from work and are reading a magazine instead.
- When you check your email, you have walked away from your work and up to your letterbox, collected your mail and opened it and started composing responses.

You wouldn't do this in any other job and expect to get things completed. In all these examples, not only have you stopped writing, but you've stopped thinking about your writing. You've killed your flow.

Simply reframing your internet procrastination as wandering away from your work can really help. When your mouse is hovering over that Chrome logo, you must say to yourself sharply, 'Don't get up. Don't walk away. Be here in the story.' The internet will wait for you. And the animals are never that funny anyway. Except that sneezing baby panda. He's awesome.

The Joys Of Being A Plotter

This was my speech for a debate about plotting versus pantsing, at the first ever Genrecon in Western Sydney, 2012.

Exhibit A: what if what you are looking at is not a glass of water, but a poorly planned ice sculpture?

Pantsing is better than plotting? Are you mad? Can you imagine if any other field of human endeavour throughout history thought this was a good idea?

- Bridge design. 'Ah let's just chuck up some poles and gaff a few popsicle sticks together and see where it takes us, hey? We don't want to be too anal.'
- Psychiatric experiments. 'Oh, just poke them a bit with electric rods and write down what happens, and we'll see if something emerges and if not, well… no great harm done, right?'
- Brain surgery. Let me tell you, there weren't enough marshmallows and tomato sauce sachets for me to make my unplanned brain surgery exhibit.

Why should writing be any different? Do you want your stories to resemble a bucket of beige slop with sickly curds floating in it and some kind of fart-smelling froth on top? Ladies and gentlemen, the difference between plotting and pantsing is the difference between success and disaster, between the sublime and the abject.

Pantsers are an odd bunch of people. They like to paint their laziness as noble unconventionality. They say stuff like, 'But plotting is so uncreative,' in between harvesting their mung beans and knitting their own yoghurt. I'd like to remind them that I still make my stories up. Being a plotter doesn't mean you've succumbed to some evil overlord who chains you into your office chair and kills puppies if you don't do as you're told. It just means that you can consider the ideas more carefully, place them more precisely, and overuse your adverbs more thoughtfully.

The other panster go-to move is, 'How do you motivate yourself to write once you know what happens?' To which I'd respond, 'How do you motivate yourself to do all that editing once you've written a big amorphous turd?' By then, you also know what happens, and you've got to wrestle with it for months if not years. By contrast, plotters write stories that, like well-formed stools, come out the right shape and the right colour with minimal clean-up required. And don't tell me you don't know the value in life of a well-formed stool.

I sense the room would rather I moved on to a more palatable metaphor, so here it is. Writing is like travelling. Pantsers are those people who say, 'Oh I just like to put on a backpack and see where the spirit takes me.' Plotters are those people who book their connecting flights and take the stress out of travel. Pantsing is, in effect, turning up at the airport and choosing a plane based on its colour; spending too much of your money on it and not really knowing where you might land; finding yourself in a city where you don't speak the language and then wandering the streets for hours looking for a nice place to stay, to find the last vacancy is in a hotel on a street where cars are regularly set fire. There you climb up the eight flights of stairs to your crusty room, only to find there are pubes on the sheets and you can hear the guy in the next room pissing.

Plotting, however, is knowing where you're going to go

before you leave the house; packing appropriately, knowing how much to budget so you don't run out of money before you come home, and then stepping on to a German Intercity Express train. It's really fast, it's super comfortable, it's even a little sexy.

And it arrives on your editor's desk, precisely on time.

Your Writing Fitness

About a year ago, without really intending to, I started to get fit. I am a girl with a permanent moontan who has spent a great deal of her life in libraries, so don't underestimate how unusual it is in my profession to be physically active or outdoorsy. It started with me buying a bicycle, then deciding I was going to ride it to the top of the mountain near my house. It took a few months for me to get all the way to the top (up the easy side), and then another few to make it regularly all the way around, then a few more to make it up the hard side and around (which is now my regular route). Because I started to get muscles in my legs and feared looking like a Tyrannosaurus, I then signed up with an exercise physiologist to do some upper body work once a week, then did a bit more of that, got back into my pilates, decided to learn to swim, and so on. It was kind of an avalanche of physical activity and I certainly feel wonderful for it (especially boxing; lord how I love boxing). My back has never been better and I've put on 4kg of lean muscle (still can't get lids off jars though) and my resting heart rate is 58 beats per minute. I like to imagine my heart looking like Conan, pumping out such a big whoosh of bubbling blood every second that it can rest and pick its teeth in between.

But this isn't about physical fitness, it's about writing fitness. While riding my bike around and around that mountain, I have had plenty of time to reflect on my writing and about writing habits in general. These are the five lessons about writing fitness I have learned from regular exercise.

1. A 6-week binge won't improve your skills measurably and permanently. You need to do a little every day if you want results. Think sustainable, not grandiose goals that won't stick.
2. There is always somebody faster than you. Don't compete with them.
3. There is always somebody who seems to get to the top of the hill with much less effort than you. Sometimes it's because they have an advantage, like a personal mentor, or a family who have encouraged them since birth, or expensive equipment. Don't compare yourself to them.
4. Your writing fitness will be apparent in more than just measurable goals such as word count. It will be in nuanced craft things that you don't notice at first, but which start to come naturally and readily where they didn't before.
5. Find a way to enjoy the process rather than solely being motivated by the outcome.

Go on; just do it.

Multi-millionaire

On August 31 2012, I will launch my 22nd book, *Lighthouse Bay*, under the name Kimberley Freeman. I have done the maths, and calculated that the release of this book will see me pass two million words of fiction in print. From the age of 4 (if not before), I knew I wanted to be a writer, though I never imagined I'd have two million words in print one day, especially as I'm not yet (I hope) halfway through life. That means there's every chance that I might make it to five million before I pop my clogs.

Still. Something about the passing of this milestone has given me a new feeling of knowing everything. Okay, technically I can't know everything. But I feel like I do anyway. Like, if you asked me any question at all about writing fiction, I would answer you immediately, thoroughly, informatively, and be 100% confident I was right. After all, I am the two-million-word girl.

So here is my best advice for fiction writing distilled. (There are swears. I grew up swearing a lot in the outer suburbs and I used to be embarrassed about that, but now I'm rocking my outer-suburbs upbringing because I'm a fucking expert now and nobody can say welfare class girls can't do it.)

1. Write, you muthafucka! Write the fucking fiction!

Don't write blogs and marketing plans and twitter yourself in front of everyone in hopes of building a platform. Write the fucking fiction FIRST. The rest is just white noise until you have a good, finished product. And it must be good. We live in an instant gratification society. You can post some nonsense while sitting on the toilet on Facebook and seventeen people can "like" it before you've wiped your arse. That's not going to cut it in the world of writing fiction. You need to shape, craft, edit, prune, elaborate, make the writing BEAUTIFUL. Then, and only then, can you hold your head high in a public forum and say, 'I am a writer. I write beautifully. You will know my name.'

2. Extreme love or go home. Don't write to impress your father/your teacher/the literati/the fickle marketplace. Write something that comes from deep, deep down. Haul it wriggling its slimy tentacles into the light, and pin it on the page with passion and precision and care and EXTREME LOVE. It's really hard to write a book. Why the fuck would you write one you didn't love EXTREMELY? It'd be more fun to pull your own eyeballs out on corn skewers. And you know what the world doesn't need more of: careless art tossed off cynically. Don't you know that it's a fool who plays it cool, by making the world a little colder? Or so the Beatles said.

3. Never compare yourself to other people. Never. It is futile, exhausting, and poisons you to the point where you don't know what you extreme-love anymore. So somebody in your writers' group got published ahead of you? SO FUCKING WHAT? Are you dead? Then quit complaining. If you think that somebody else's success makes you small, then you are telling yourself your stories don't matter. They do. Write your stories, from your heart; and if you have followed steps one

and two, they will be precious and meaningful and belong in the world, even if the only audience they ever meet is a small one.

4. And all this is true, I know, because I am a fucking expert and I am always right.

The Craft Of Writing

Plot Versus Character

From time to time, aspiring writers ask me what is the best kind of story: one that is plot-driven or one that is character-driven? Somehow the idea that the two are distinct and one can be privileged over the other persists. 'Character-driven' is usually seen as the mark of serious writing, while 'plot-driven' is understood to be written by hacks pandering to the marketplace. This is a false distinction, and a potentially dangerous one at that. No writer can afford to overlook one or the other: a good story is driven by both good plot ideas and good characters. The trick is managing them right.

1. A story isn't a story until it has *people* and *problems*. These two things (character and plot) cannot in any way be conceived outside of each other. An idea for a fascinating character means little until that character is challenged in some way; and a high-stakes plot idea means little if it isn't focalised through three-dimensional people whose thoughts and feelings can be communicated to the reader.

2. What the writer must know first and foremost is the relationship between the people and the problems. Why is this person involved in this problem? Is it random? Or is it a function of the very person they

are? What kind of attempts do they make to solve the problem, and where do those attempted solutions lead them? You must always think of the problem as *belonging* to somebody: a story describes that relationship between people and their problems.

3. Use the problems to create the narrative steps. How is your character going to get out of their predicament? What new problems can arise? The problems create the horizontal movement of the story, from beginning, through middle, and to the end; the movement that sustains narrative interest and keeps your reader turning pages. In some respects, the plot is driven by character: it evolves uniquely from the people and their responses to the problem they were given on page one.

4. Use the people to create the emotional connection. How does it feel to experience this problem? What history of acts and ideas does the character bring to the problem at hand? What do they think of their problem? This creates the vertical depth of your story; the depth that makes the story emotionally meaningful to your reader. In some respects, the characters are driven by the plot: they evolve uniquely from the narrative trajectory, which brings about their transformation from the person they were on page one, to the person they are when you write 'the end'.

Building Blocks

The building blocks of a story are scenes. The term 'scene' is borrowed from drama, and it can be useful to conceive of your story this way. The set goes up, the lights come on, the action and dialogue happen. Then the set is struck and the next one goes up, and so on. Writing a story, even a really long story such as a novel or a trilogy or a septology or a *Wheel of Time*, is simply a matter of writing one scene at a time until you finish (or die). It can be really helpful, then, to think through what each scene will do before you write it:

1. Scenes can move the narrative forward. Actually, I want to say that scenes *should always* move the narrative forward, but I don't want to be prescriptive. This is the most important and obvious function a scene has: simply working through the various stages of the characters' problems and solutions in a cause-and-effect chain. This is how a story gains its forward motion. If you have a slow story, perhaps it's because there are too many scenes that don't create narrative interest. *But* simply moving the narrative forward is not enough. Scenes can work much harder than that.

2. Scenes help flesh out the world of your story. In most scenes you can add some detail and depth to the

setting, maybe fill in background and history, to create a feeling of a solid and realistic fictional world.

3. Scenes help flesh out your characters. Each scene gives you an opportunity to show what your characters will or won't do, to detail how they react under pressure, to explore the characters' inner worlds of thoughts and feelings. By doing this, you draw the reader closer to your characters and create a connection that will keep your readers interested.

4. Scenes are great for moderating pace. Perhaps you've just written back-to-back helicopter chases. Now, instead of jumping straight into a car chase, perhaps you should stop and write a scene that creates intimacy with the characters, or creates a complementary mood or atmosphere. It gives readers a breather, reconnects them to the human aspect of the story, and gives them the energy for the next big action scene.

5. Scenes can simply exist to show off your writing. Perhaps you want to write a poetic and ambitious set-piece in which the themes of your story are crystallised in a metaphoric, rather than literal, way. This is the kind of device that can work magnificently, but probably shouldn't be overused.

Of course, a good scene is a hard-working one that performs as many of these functions as it comfortably can. Scenes that work hard make for a tight, focussed story; and help you organise your story from beginning to end.

Narrative Structure

Stories should have a beginning, middle, and end, and managing the proportions of those parts is crucial for pleasing and persuasive pace, especially in the novel. A story has a rhythm: a set-up, a development, a resolution. Think of the Freudian ideas of the pleasure principle and the death drive: narrative structure can be seen as an interplay between the desire to be lost in pleasure and the desire to return to an inert state. We all know the intense gratification of being in the midst of a huge novel, wanting it to go on forever; and yet at the same time finding ourselves unable to stop turning the pages and racing towards the resolution. This rhythm plays to the expectations of the reader: there is a lot of enjoyment to be gained from a well-managed three-part structure.

The three parts—beginning, middle, end—have different functions (introducing, developing, and resolving) and should represent different proportions of the story. Of course this is not an exact science, but:

- The beginning should take up the first twenty to thirty percent of the word count.
- The middle should take up roughly half.
- The remainder should be assigned to the ending.

Sticking to these proportions will help you avoid a beginning that drags halfway into the book, or an ending that is all over too quickly. Readers can enjoy the set-up, take their pleasure stuck in the middle for a long time, and then be pulled through on the tide of the end. These ideas rely on there being relatively clear transition points, at least for the writer, between the beginning and middle, and the middle and end. These transition points are like gear changes in the narrative structure: if you listen closely enough, you will nearly always hear them in good storytelling.

- The first transition point is an indicator that the story has kicked off and is ready to be developed. Take Shakespeare's *Macbeth*, for example. The beginning of the story introduces us to Macbeth and his wife, to the prophecy of the witches, and the plan for murder. Macbeth kills Duncan one-fifth of the way into the story (at the end of act one), signalling the end of the beginning.
- The second transition point is an indicator that matters have become so intense as to force an ending either way. A Rubicon is crossed, a die is cast, a watershed moment is reached: the amount of clichés available to me here demonstrates just how entrenched the idea of a point-of-no-return is in narrative. When Macbeth returns to the witches and consciously aligns himself with evil, we hear the gear change clearly: the ending is rushing upon us now.
- Once you know what these transition points are, you have the spine of the story. Writing it is simply a matter of negotiating the distance between the points with scenes. Easy!

Managing Scope

Stories come in all lengths, but it can be hard to judge the scope of a story before you start writing it. You might find as you write that the story is pulling up too short, or going on far too long.

- Consider your form. A short story simply can't deal with too many ideas. A novel has to represent nuance and complexity. If you misjudge, you might end up with a novella. Now, novellas are fine and dandy but hard to find a market for.
- Consider your genre. These things aren't set in stone, but audiences expect certain word lengths in certain genres. Epic high fantasy, for example, is usually long. Literary fiction, by contrast, is often short.
- Consider your target age group: Generally speaking, novels for children and young adult are shorter than novels written for adults.

So, what do you do if your first draft of a historical epic for adults is only 40,000 words long?

- Look for a character with potential for development. What is their version of the story? Could it make a worthy subplot?

- Check that you haven't rushed the plot. The tension should rise slowly over the course of the story: perhaps you've simply peaked too soon, and need to go back and write a few "spacer" scenes.
- Look for scenes where you have summarised and see if you can dramatise instead. Sometimes in our hurry to get things down, we don't take the time to lay out details. For example, 'Frodo took the ring to Mount Doom' cuts out a lot of interesting action.

Conversely, what do you do if your young adult romance clocks in at 250 000 words?

- Check that you haven't started the story too early. A story should start with a point of strong narrative interest, not with acres of character history.
- Reduce the amount of viewpoint characters. Do you really need all of those perspectives on the action?
- Cut all repetition. Look for characters who perform similar functions, scenes that describe similar actions, even sentences that say the same thing twice.
- Look at every scene and decide whether or not it's contributing meaningfully to the progress of the story. Those that don't will have to go.

Of course, a story is as long as it is, and you shouldn't feel you have to cut out important things, or puff it up with irrelevant subplots. But if you are determined to be published consider the expectations of your reader, and don't wear out your welcome or abandon them too soon.

Four Ways To Get To Know Your Characters

When embarking on a story, writers often agonise over their characters. It takes a while for a clear sense of them to emerge, and they seem always poised to fall into stereotype. Try these methods to flesh your characters out.

1. FEARS AND DESIRES

To start with, you need to know the character's greatest fear, and their greatest desire. These are what I call the 'big engines' that drive characters at a fundamental level. But don't ask your characters to tell you, as often they won't even know what their greatest fears or desires are, let alone be able or willing to articulate them. Those things might be secret, or unacknowledged, or repressed. (Yes, yes, I *know* they're not real people).

2. TO LIST OR NOT TO LIST?

How-to-write books often suggest that you make lists of character traits. While there's no great harm in doing this, these abstract facts are meaningless in themselves. If you decide that your protagonist is a Catholic socialist whose favourite colour is yellow, you don't necessarily know him or her any better. Far more interesting is the character's *relationship* with those traits. That is, how does the character feel about being a Catholic and a socialist? Does he talk about socialism in church? And how does yellow make him feel? What associations does it have for him? Use character traits as prompts to think about deeper complexities.

3. OFF-STAGE LIFE

Sometimes you'll read a book where it seems the characters pop out of the box for their scenes, then go back into it when they're not required. Instead, aim to give a sense that the characters have something to do when they're not 'on-stage': that way they seem real and textured. Photocopy a blank diary page and nut out — hour by hour — what your character does in a typical week. Sure they will sleep: but how long? What time do they get up? Do they work? What kind of tasks do they perform? Do they eat regular meals? And so on. You can gain great insight into a character this way, even if you never use most of the information you create.

4. WRITE YOUR WAY IN

Really, the best way to understand your characters is to write about them. It's like any relationship: spending extended time with somebody is the only authentic way to get to know them, and it can't be forced. You must be brave enough to write your way into their heads and hearts, and trust that by the end of the story you'll know them well enough to come back and fix the beginning.

Your Supporting Cast

Most of us understand what it takes to make the central characters in a story work. We know we have to develop motivations, shade in the greys, and ensure that they have three dimensions so that they are real and convincing to the reader. But there are many more characters in your story than just the central ones, and it's very easy to slip into bad habits with your supporting cast: that's where you'll find your snooping secretaries, your cowboys with black hats, and your whores with hearts of gold. Turning your spotlight on your supporting cast, so that they can be just as well-rounded and complex as your central characters, will mean your whole story benefits. Here are some key questions to ask yourself, to see if your supporting cast are pulling their weight.

- I've borrowed the term 'supporting cast' from film, and it's helpful to ask yourself this of your secondary characters: if somebody was playing this part in a film, would the actor have enough material to work with to win a best supporting actor Oscar? If it helps, think of a really fine actor in the part: an Olivia Coleman or an Idris Elba. Is there something for them to sink their teeth into? If the answer is no, then read on.
- Write a list of your secondary characters. Who are

they? And by that, I don't mean for you merely to describe them (eg. 'Larry's wife'). I mean, *what role* do they play in the story? What is their function in relation to the central characters of the story (eg. 'the person who most wants to find out Larry's secrets')? Immediately, you'll see who has fallen into stereotype, or is behaving in a baffling manner, or who is just plain boring.

- Once you've clarified these roles, start giving the character the kind of attention you'd ordinarily give to central characters. How well do you know them? Could you name their greatest fear? Their most burning desire?

- Allow yourself to imagine for a little while that this story is actually *their* story, rather than the central character's. What light does this exercise shed on the story, and on the secondary character's relationship to the story? You don't have to include this perspective in the story, but you should know it for yourself. It will help you make the secondary character's actions and reactions more consistent and convincing.

- Most importantly, make sure you really know why the character acts the way they do in this story. Their motivation should be internal, arising from their unique personalities; not external, arising at the author's convenience.

A supporting cast really does help hold up the central characters. Central characters who are brilliantly developed will suffer if the story is flimsy beneath them. If secondary characters are lavished with the same kind of development — even if a great deal of that background information never makes it on to the page — the central characters have a secure place to stand.

World Building

The biggest challenge of all facing fantasy writers, is how to build an entire secondary fantastic world. This skill, known as 'world building', is far more difficult than popular opinion might have it. There is no 'just making it up'. A secondary fantasy world must cohere logically and convincingly, must be fully mapped in time and space, and must be integrated at all levels with the lives of the characters who people it. This daunting task is best broken down into three processes: reading, living, and writing.

READING

Take in information that can inspire ideas for how the secondary world operates. Don't just read inside the genre to adapt what other writers have done: do some research. If your fantasy novel is set in a faux-medieval world, read up on the actual medieval period; or approach science fiction via a curious reading of scientific research rather than a brief review of the *Star Wars* movies. That is not to say that fantasy fiction is only worthy if it is historically accurate, or science fiction is only worthy if it is 'hard' science fiction, but broaden your horizons at the development phase and it will pay off in scope later on.

LIVING

World building does not have to be approached from the outside in: that is, starting with geography, history, religion, etc. It can usefully be approached from the inside out: that is, starting with a character and tracking that character through a typical day of life as it is lived, to discover which aspects of the world are most important to develop for the story's purposes. A fun way to approach this task is to take a notebook with you for the day and write down everything you do. From this list, you begin to map your character's day. 'I had breakfast' translates into a series of questions about breakfast in your secondary world, common foods, their source, how they are grown or transported, how they are received culturally, and so on. Many budding fantasy writers fill notebooks with details about their secondary worlds, but until those facts are mobilised in relationships with characters, they remain abstract. The danger also exists that, because the writer has taken the time to develop the ideas, they must appear somewhere in the story even if they don't naturally fit. Remember: serve the story before you serve yourself.

WRITING

Make journeys into your secondary world before it is properly 'finished'. Until you actually start writing about your characters in your world, you won't know what details you might need. Treat writing as a reconnaissance mission: when you hit a white space, it is time to go back to the world building. Your secondary world is provisional right up until it goes into print: the process of reading, living, and writing is iterative. You cycle through and repeat, through first and second drafts and beyond. Eventually, you will know that secondary world as well as you know your own.

Orient And Anchor

One of the biggest problems people have with setting their scenes is the right amount of description. Is there too much? Is there too little? The first (too much) is an easy prospect to fix:

1. Check your descriptions. Remove all repetitions, and break up all chunks longer than four sentences. You want to avoid setting up with a long, detailed description (like a backdrop) then moving into the action (like a foreground): that feels stagey and not real.
2. Consider your genre: a historical novel thrives on rich detail; a thriller can be sparser; a fantasy novel needs to explain things enough to get a picture.
3. Consider who the description is serving: you or the reader? You should aim to serve the reader. We have a word in the Australian vernacular for people who please themselves.

Most writers actually give us too little description, especially when it's an exotic or unusual setting. It creates that annoying problem we call 'white space'. Action and dialogue are happening, but they seem detached from the surroundings. The reader can't visualise the scene, and so it loses its impact and invites skimming. Two words that can really help you here are *orient* and *anchor*. In each scene, you should aim to orient the reader quickly, then anchor the setting securely in their imagination.

1. Within the first two paragraphs of a scene, earlier if possible, you should orient the reader. Where are we? Is it day or night? Inside or outside? Are there crowds of people around, or nobody? And, of course, whose head are we in?

2. Within one double-spaced page, earlier if possible, you should put in a set of anchor points using specific images: cobbled street, brightly painted shutters, noisy market stalls; tall gum trees, muddy creek, churning storm clouds; polished mahogany desk, white leather armchair, sombre-coloured roman blinds. It's okay to cluster them tightly together, but do it with a light touch. These anchor points begin to map the white space for your reader: already they are starting to see and feel the setting.

3. How much you add now depends on your genre. Start evoking the other senses in little beats: the smell of lemons and rosemary from the fruit stall; the sticky blanket of humidity; the expectant ticking of a clock. These beats are spread throughout the action, are part of the narrative rather than standing outside it. A little here, a little there.

4. Now make sure these evocative beats are attached to a viewpoint character. You are recording the effect of the setting on somebody's senses and somebody's thoughts. Then it feels more real for the reader.

5. Hey, presto! You've set a scene!

What To Do About Clichés

The problem with clichés is that they are often not noticeable: writers think they'd know one because it's obvious: 'she thanked her lucky stars'; 'he had a heart of gold'. They'd never use one of those tired old expressions! But new clichés are being made all the time: 'dealt a savage blow', 'sorely mistaken', 'grim determination', 'dripping with sarcasm'. All of these are clichés, and all of them are in frequent use in fiction. The faster you write, the more likely you are to reach for a cliché as a shortcut. Readers don't engage with clichés, and too many can make writing seem tired and boring. Remember though, that clichés are overused because they work well. That is, most clichés were originally very good ideas. But like a rock being rolled around in the sea, it eventually loses its texture and becomes smooth (which is why they often go unnoticed).

- First, train yourself to identify a cliché. It's usually figurative. For example, 'sorely mistaken': mistakes are not usually physically painful so this adds the idea of metaphorical physical pain to a mistake. It's a way of intensifying the mistakenness. Often the best way to identify a cliché, though, is simply to ask yourself if this collection of words has appeared together in this order many times before.

- It can help to think back to the original sentiment of the cliché. Ask yourself, what was originally interesting or fresh about it? Can you write that original interest back in, a different way? e.g. 'glowing reviews' – the idea is that the reviews contain so much praise they emit light. Can you reconfigure? 'Reviews bright enough to read by'?
- Or perhaps you don't need the cliché at all, you might not want to draw that much attention to something which is a side detail: 'good reviews' or 'excellent reviews' can work just fine. So another option is to scale the cliché back to literality.
- Remember too, that some clichés are so time-honoured that they can continue in use and bother few people; they've become almost as invisible as if they were literal. I've yet to find a better way to say 'burst into tears' or 'her heart sank'.
- Also, sometimes characters talk in clichés. An unimaginative character may very well say 'for the umpteenth time', and it's appropriate to characterise them in this manner.
- It's useful to think of clichés as band-aids over gaps where something specific should have been written. When you find one, ask yourself, 'What am I *really* trying to say here?'

Clichés aren't an evil in themselves, but a flag that something evil might be going on. If you find one, consider it carefully. If it's not pulling its weight in your writing, then do something about it.

Calendar Of Events

A story outline that plots your beginning, middle, and end is very useful. But these categories are functional rather than chronological. After all, stories jump about in time, flash back and forwards, and sometimes feature whole subplots in different time periods. A helpful tool for a novelist is a calendar of events. On the calendar, you plot the events of the story in time. You can do this before, during, or after you've written a story, and it helps you get a wide view of the action, so you can see what happens when.

- Design your calendar to suit your story. If it takes place over three days, then divide the calendar into hours. If it takes place over three years, then divide it into months or seasons.
- If you are writing a story that takes place over years, it really helps to keep a list with every character's birthday on it, so you don't put an eight-year-old in a booster seat, or have a character marry at fourteen.
- Find all the unaccounted-for time. Make sure you haven't written that days have passed when it has actually been months. Do your characters have lives outside the events of the story? When do they go to work, shop, shower? You might need to account for

the missing time somehow, even if it is a quick and simple summary.

- Check on the weather. If you have your characters kissing in the snow and it's June in St Petersburg, you've got some explaining to do. Likewise, be careful about what flowers are blooming when. Sometimes in the heat of the creative moment, we might think 'gardenias! there was the smell of gardenias!' Which is great, but if it's August in Brisbane you might need jasmine instead.

- What about the moon? If you have a full moon's light shining on one scene, and then it's all dark in the next, either time has passed or there are clouds. If there are a lot of outdoor night scenes, you may have to keep track of moon phases. That kind of work is better done before the edit than after, obviously.

- Look out for evidence of the writer/character time disjunction. It can take you weeks as an author to work through a chapter, even if that chapter only covers a few days of action in your story. In my first novel, I spent months carefully building the romantic tension between two characters as they slowly got to know each other, then had them finally fall in love despite their reservations. When I read it back and plotted it on a calendar, it had taken place over two days.

- If you write historical fiction, make sure you mark in important historical events. Even if you don't intend to write about the events directly, they may have an impact on the characters' lives.

Writing a novel is a huge feat of project management, and a calendar of events is just one way to get your head around the story so that it's plausible and consistent.

Precision Editing

Few things are more daunting than embarking on the first self-edit of your novel. You can get swamped in an edit very easily so it is vital that you cultivate above all the ability to be *methodical* and *detached*. Editing your novel is like autopsying a puppy. It's hard to put aside your feelings and start cutting, but if you can't be methodical and detached, then more puppies may die.

1. First, print out the manuscript and get it away from your computer. Go through it with a pen, marking anything you feel needs fixing. Importantly, don't try to fix it on the first pass. Separate out the processes of identifying problems and fixing problems. Certainly, if you know the perfect substitute word put it in, but a little note to yourself such as 'this paragraph is vague' will suffice. If you like, you can imagine you are not the person who has to fix it. Take the pressure off.

2. Next, take your manuscript back to your computer and, starting at page one, work through the problems you've noted, without reading the manuscript. Just work through the notes in order. Do the easy ones right away (e.g. typos, deletions, small rewrites). Don't fix the ones that are more complex or require more time. Instead, mark them with a note (I used the

'review' menu in Word) and keep moving through. Once you get to the end of the MS, you can count up your notes. Don't be daunted if there are hundreds; that is certainly not unusual.

3. These notes are now your agenda. Don't read the novel again, just move from comment to comment, working on the screen, methodically fixing them one at a time. You don't have to work in order now. Leave the hard or large problems and fix the easy ones first so you get a sense of satisfaction, seeing the number grow smaller and smaller.

4. For those big structural issues, isolate the sections that need to be worked on. For example, if you feel you lack good world building at the start of the novel, isolate the relevant group of scenes and then read through them again, weaving in an extra line here and there. Or if you feel a character is acting awkwardly or without enough motivation, isolate the chapters where you feel the problem is most acute and make a note for each scene about the character's feelings and reactions. If you feel you need a whole new scene, put in another note to return to.

5. When you are done, print the manuscript and repeat until you are satisfied.

Remember, the problems are always in the words. All you are really doing is getting rid of the ones that don't work, and putting in ones that do. In a methodical and detached way.

Keep Going

Novels are a long haul. If you are working on one, at some point it's almost guaranteed that you'll find it hard to keep going. Once you stop working consistently, you can fall out of your story making it doubly hard to get back in. Here are some ideas to help you get going again.

1. Work out whether you've stopped writing for practical or for psychological reasons. Not writing because your study is being renovated is quite different from not writing because you have lost faith in your abilities. Identifying what kind of problem you're having helps you develop an appropriate solution: do you need to find a library you can work in until renovations are finished, or do you need to find somebody who will listen and encourage you?

2. Have a notebook for your ideas and open it every day for at least 10 minutes. I know a lot of people use computer software for organising their ideas, but there's simply no substitute for an old-fashioned notebook: completely portable, doesn't need plugging in, and provides a wonderful tactile sensation (mmm ... new stationery...). Once you have it open, you don't have to do anything but look — I don't even mind if

you have the TV on while you do it. It's an effective way to keep in touch with your novel without any pressure. Pen in hand, please! Ideas *always* come.

3. Go to other media for inspiration. Make a playlist of songs that suit the feel of the novel, find some art that inspires you, or go and see a movie in the same genre. Might any of these things be a good prompt for some free writing? For example, you could put on a piece of music and scribble down random words and phrases. None of it may make its way into the story, but at least you're writing again.

4. Enlist a cheer squad. Your family, your friends, your writing buddies, all want you to keep going too. Set up some group pomodoros[1] with writing friends, promise your best friend to give them a chapter by the end of the week, or update your social media to say you aren't allowed back on until you've written 1000 words, and see how quickly people rush to support you. It's hard to let them down when they've shown so much faith in you.

5. Indulge yourself with some uninterrupted daydreaming. Schedule some time when you can be alone with your imagination for a whole hour. Daydream about your cover blurb, what scene you'll read at your book launch, your reviews, who might be cast in the movie. This isn't idle daydreaming: thinking about the reception of your novel will help you clarify what kind of novel you want it to be.

6. Write. Because in the end, that's all you need to do.

---

1. From Francesco Cirillo's popular Pomodoro Technique. A pomodoro means setting a timer and working through four blocks of 25 minutes, with a 5-minute break between each block.

About the Author

Kim Wilkins was born in London, and grew up at the seaside north of Brisbane, Australia. She is a Professor of Writing and Publishing at The University of Queensland. She has published more than thirty novels and her work has been translated into more than twenty languages. She has two delightful teenage children, a very hunky husband who is also a doctor, and an unkickable Reddit habit. Kim has enduring obsessions with Viking-age England, misty landscapes, pagan mythology, Led Zeppelin, and really really small dogs.

Also by Kim Wilkins

Adult Fantasy

Queens of the Sea

Sisters of the Fire

The Silver Well (with Kate Forsyth)

Odin's Girl

Daughters of the Storm

The Year of Ancient Ghosts

Rosa and the Veil of Gold

Giants of the Frost

The Autumn Castle

Angel of Ruin

The Resurrectionists

Grimoire

The Infernal

Women's Historical Adventures (by Kimberley Freeman)

Stars Across the Ocean

Evergreen Falls

Ember Island

Lighthouse Bay

Wildflower Hill

Gold Dust

Duet

Young Adult Novels

The Pearl Hunters
Nightshade: A Gina Champion Mystery
Witchsong: A Gina Champion Mystery
Moonstorm: A Gina Champion Mystery
Fireheart: A Gina Champion Mystery
Bloodlace: A Gina Champion Mystery

Children's Books

Ghost Ship: The Sunken Kingdom I
Tide Stealers: The Sunken Kingdom II
Sorcerer of the Waves: The Sunken Kingdom III
The Star Queen: The Sunken Kingdom IV
Space Boogers

Thank You For Buying This Brain Jar Press Chapbook

To receive special offers, bonus content, and info on new releases and other great reads, visit us online at www.BrainJarPress.com

www.ingramcontent.com/pod-product-compliance
Lightning Source LLC
Chambersburg PA
CBHW022106020426
42335CB00012B/852